ET TU, BRUTE?

ET TU, BRUTE?

THE DEATHS OF THE ROMAN EMPERORS

JASON NOVAK

W. W. NORTON & COMPANY
Independent Publishers Since 1923
NEW YORK | LONDON

For information about permission to reproduce selections from this book, write to
Permissions, W. W. Norton & Company, Inc., 500 Fifth Avenue, New York, NY 10110

For information about special discounts for bulk purchases, please contact
W. W. Norton Special Sales at specialsales@wwnorton.com or 800-233-4830

Manufacturing by Versa Press
Production manager: Beth Steidle

Library of Congress Cataloging-in-Publication Data

Names: Novak, Jason, 1979– author.
Title: Et tu, Brute? : the deaths of the Roman emperors / Jason Novak.
Description: First edition. | New York : W. W. Norton & Company, 2018.
Identifiers: LCCN 2017054871 | ISBN 9780393635737 (hardcover)
Subjects: LCSH: Emperors—Rome—Death—Caricatures and cartoons. |
Emperors—Rome—Biography—Caricatures and cartoons. | American wit
and humor, Pictorial.
Classification: LCC DG274 .N68 2018 | DDC 937/.060922—dc23
LC record available at https://lccn.loc.gov/2017054871

W. W. Norton & Company, Inc., 500 Fifth Avenue, New York, N.Y. 10110
www.wwnorton.com

W. W. Norton & Company Ltd., 15 Carlisle Street, London W1D 3BS

1 2 3 4 5 6 7 8 9 0

To Gertrude and Eloise,
but don't try this at home.

O, Death
O, Death
Won't you spare me over 'til another year
Won't you spare me over 'til another year
Won't you spare me over 'til another year

—traditional, arranged by
the Stanley Brothers

Introduction

BEING AN EMPEROR in ancient Rome was a dangerous business. In the abstract, it sounds like a great gig, but it wasn't all bacchanalias and parties in the Hippodrome; it was a horrible job filled with violence and treachery. The emperor's survival was predicated on an unthinkable (to us, at least) level of personal and public brutality. Even Marcus Aurelius, known to posterity for his collection of ascetic philosophical analects—a philosopher king, as it were—bloodied his hands in endless border wars with Germany and Persia.

Warfare was a major killer of emperors. In an age when leadership prided itself on foolhardy bravery, emperors and generals participated fully in hand-to-hand combat alongside their armies. Many emperors disappeared in the fray of battle, and it must be assumed they perished under the blade of the enemy.

Treachery was another major cause of death. For example, in 54 AD the emperor Claudius was poisoned by his own wife so that her son from a previous marriage (the infamous Nero) could inherit the throne. Later, in 192

AD, the mad emperor Commodus, who fancied himself a gladiator, was strangled to death by his longtime wrestling companion. Quite a few emperors were killed by their own generals while on military campaigns.

The rare emperor lucky enough to avoid being killed in battle or murdered by someone who wanted the job faced death by any number of gruesome maladies. One common but now very treatable illness was dropsy, also known as edema—a chronic inflammation of the extremities. As if illness weren't enough, sometimes the treatments were even deadlier. A few emperors died at the hands of well-meaning but ignorant physicians.

✦ ✦ ✦

ET TU, BRUTE? is an illustrated compendium of the deaths of the Roman emperors from the establishment of the Roman Empire to the fall of Rome. Contrary to popular assumption, the first emperor was not Julius Caesar but his adopted nephew Octavian, who later styled himself Augustus. Julius Caesar was merely a consul—a sort of senatorial whip in a government without a head of state. He proclaimed himself a provisional dictator during a time of national crisis, effectively setting the parameters of what would eventually become the role of emperor. But Caesar himself was assassinated by his cohorts in the Senate before the role of emperor was codified.

The title of this book is a line from Shakespeare's *Julius Caesar*. Shakespeare was paraphrasing a line from Plutarch's account of Julius Caesar's assassination, where Caesar is stabbed to death by his friends in the Senate and sees his closest compatriot among them, a man named Brutus. "And you, too, Brutus?" he says in Latin. I like the idea of having Julius Caesar as a ghost in the book—a force that's felt but not seen.

With Augustus, Rome was for the first time embodied in a single person. The story of an emperor's life became the story of Rome. And the death of any given emperor tells us, in an encapsulated way, what was happening in the empire generally. By the reign of Constantine, which began in 306 AD, the empire had been split into two (and sometimes three) administrative districts, which were ruled at any given time by multiple co-emperors and vice emperors.

Et Tu, Brute? ends with the collapse of the western Roman Empire. The eastern empire continued for another thousand years, but the birthplace of the empire, the city of Rome itself, was irrevocably overrun by barbarians in 476 AD, when Romulus Augustulus was emperor.

So, from Augustus to Romulus Augustulus, this book includes all of the emperors and co-emperors who were officially recognized by the Roman Senate (a mere formality, but still to be distinguished from pretenders and usurpers). I've included a few extras who might be interesting to modern readers, like the empress Zenobia, a usurper from Persia, and one of the few women in the history of the empire to reign solo, without a man taking all the credit. It should be noted that many emperors turned to their wives and mothers to make administrative and military decisions—a fact not lost when an emperor's wife or mother was murdered during a rebellion.

As to the particular cause of each emperor's death, in general I've tried to be true to what we know of Roman history. For much information I depended on Michael Grant's *The Roman Emperors: A Biographical Guide to the Rulers of Imperial Rome*. But in places where Grant was vague or unsatisfying about imperial deaths, I went to primary sources: Herodian's *History of the Empire from the Death of Marcus*, Ammianus Marcellinus's *The Later Roman Empire*, and the anonymous *Augustan History*. The last is the most fun to read, because it's crammed with flagrant, scandalous lies. Naturally I found it the most inspiring.

In three cases where historians had no conclusive information about a death or the temerity to make one up, I took gross liberties. I've shown the boy emperor Diadumenian getting bludgeoned to death by a tree stump, for example. That is pure invention on my part. Not only have no emperors been implicated in tree stump bludgeonings, I haven't been able to pull up any instances of tree stump bludgeonings anywhere in the ancient world. Modern instances are mostly logging accidents.

In another instance, I've drawn Philip the Arab getting sliced completely in half, from nape to navel. It's utter fabrication on my part. We don't know how he was killed. But my fabrication is less absurd than many of the death stories cooked up by ancient historians.

And, finally, I show Gordian III having his entire skeleton pulled out through the top of his head, which is physically impossible.

To inform my drawings I've also used the busts that, until around the third century AD, most Roman emperors had made of their likeness. Thereafter the empire was in such a bad way that most often the only idea we have of imperial likenesses comes from portraits on the coins minted during an emperor's reign. Though more formulaic, they do still convey some idea about changing fashions in head and neckwear, and I've reflected that in my drawings.

As Rome grew in size and diversity, the classical image we have of starkly adorned senators in spare white togas gave way to a strange combination of the rough leggings and capes of tribal Germans mixed with the gilded and bejeweled sensibility of the Persians. It's the nature of an empire, after years of colonial rule, to eventually assimilate some of the manners and habits of its subjected territories.

The later emperors had a whole nest of gewgaws in their hair and around their necks.

◆ ◆ ◆

IF THIS BOOK shares anything with the literary tradition of ancient Rome, it would be through satire and farce, which thrived during the Roman Republic and early Roman Empire. Roman satire was dominated by conservative voices lamenting the collapse of traditional standards. Chief among these were Horace and Juvenal, whose verse essays were conservative in their sentiment yet radical and pyrotechnic in style, much like a cartoon.

Et Tu, Brute? also has ancestors in the *memento mori* literature of the Middle Ages and Renaissance. The best-known example is Hans Holbein's *Danse Macabre*, a collection of illustrated verses showing how nobody escapes the icy clutches of death.

When I started it, I thought this book would be a straightforward illustrated guide to the deaths of Rome's emperors. I have, after all, long been fascinated by them. My first real awareness came from watching the *I, Claudius* TV miniseries, starring Derek Jacobi as the stammering emperor Claudius. I was enthralled with that show and would go around the apartment in bedsheets stuttering Jacobi's lines. I'll be glad if some readers learn some history from this book, although I'm not sure how useful such knowledge is. I like the film director Errol Morris's addendum to the old adage: "Those who don't know history are doomed to repeat it without an ironic sense of futility."

But about halfway through my work, it dawned on me that it was really about death itself. By the end, I thought perhaps that with this book I was trying to win a battle with death, or at least tame it in my imagination. Now, as I sit a few drinks deep and nearly finished with the introduction, I realize that this may really just be a way to get even with all the teachers who told me in school that drawing Romans killing one another would get me nowhere. Well, it got me this book—one I've been practicing for in one way or another since first grade.

I hope you enjoy reading *Et Tu, Brute?* as much as I enjoyed drawing it. I'm sorry about all the violence.

ET TU, BRUTE?

14 AD

AUGUSTUS WAS FED POISONED
FIGS BY HIS WIFE LIVIA.

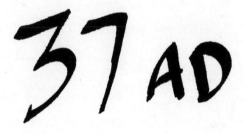

TIBERIUS WAS SMOTHERED
IN HIS SLEEP BY CALIGULA.

CALIGULA WAS STABBED THIRTY TIMES
BY THE PRAETORIAN GUARD WHILE ADDRESSING
A PLAY REHEARSAL.

54 AD

CLAUDIUS WAS FED POISONOUS MUSHROOMS
BY HIS WIFE AGRIPPINA SO HER SON NERO
COULD TAKE OVER.

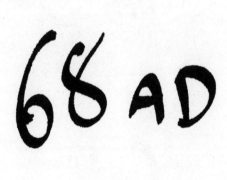

NERO STABBED HIMSELF IN THE
THROAT AFTER THE SENATE CONDEMNED
HIM TO BE FLOGGED TO DEATH.

GALBA WAS MURDERED BY PRAETORIAN
GUARDS IN THE ROMAN FORUM. HIS HEAD
WAS TAKEN TO OTHO.

69 AD

OTHO STABBED HIMSELF IN THE HEART AFTER LOSING THE BATTLE OF BEDRIACUM TO VITELLIUS.

69 AD

VITELLIUS WAS MURDERED IN THE
ROMAN FORUM BY VESPASIAN'S TROOPS
AFTER LOSING THE SECOND BATTLE
OF BEDRIACUM.

79AD

VESPASIAN DIED OF A FEVER. HIS LAST WORDS WERE "OH DEAR! I THINK I AM TURNING INTO A GOD."

TITUS WAS FED POISONED FISH
BY DOMITIAN.

DOMITIAN WAS STABBED IN THE GROIN
BY AN ASSASSIN BUT MANAGED TO KILL
HIS ASSAILANT BEFORE DYING.

98AD

NERVA DIED OF A FEVER IN HIS GARDEN.

117 AD

TRAJAN DIED OF A STROKE AFTER
QUASHING A REBELLION IN MESOPOTAMIA.

138 AD

HADRIAN DIED OF TUBERCULOSIS.

161 AD

ANTONINUS PIUS DIED AFTER GORGING
ON CHEESE. THE LAST WORD HE UTTERED
WAS "EQUANIMITY."

169 AD

LUCIUS VERUS DIED OF AN APOPLECTIC FIT.

180 AD

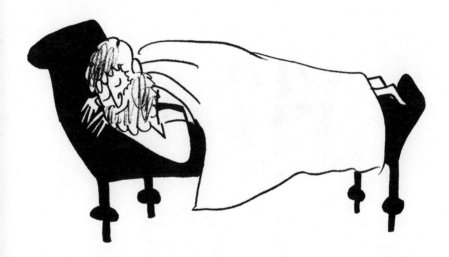

MARCUS AURELIUS DIED
PEACEFULLY IN HIS SLEEP.

192 AD

COMMODUS WAS STRANGLED TO DEATH
IN HIS BATH BY HIS WRESTLING PARTNER.

193 AD

PERTINAX WAS SPEARED IN THE
CHEST AFTER HARANGUING A CROWD
OF ANGRY SOLDIERS. HIS HEAD WAS
PARADED THROUGH THE STREETS.

193 AD

DIDIUS JULIANUS WAS KILLED BY A SOLDIER AFTER SEEKING JUSTICE FOR PERTINAX. HIS LAST WORDS WERE "BUT WHAT EVIL HAVE I DONE? WHOM HAVE I KILLED?"

194AD

PESCENNIUS NIGER, USURPER IN THE EAST, WAS KILLED ON THE RIVER EUPHRATES.

197AD

CLODIUS ALBINUS, ANOTHER USURPER, STABBED HIMSELF TO DEATH WHILE FLEEING REPRISAL.

211 AD

SEPTIMUS SEVERUS FELL ILL AND DIED WHILE
TRYING TO CONQUER SCOTLAND. HIS PARTING
WORDS WERE "BE HARMONIOUS, ENRICH THE
SOLDIERS, AND SCORN ALL OTHER MEN."

211 AD

GETA WAS MURDERED IN HIS MOTHER'S GRASP
BY CENTURIONS IN THE EMPLOY OF HIS
BROTHER, CARACALLA.

217AD

CARACALLA WAS STABBED BY A DISGRUNTLED
SOLDIER WHILE RELIEVING HIMSELF.

218 AD

MACRINUS, FACED WITH AN
UPRISING, APPOINTED HIS TEN-YEAR-OLD
SON DIADUMENIAN EMPEROR,
AND DIED WHILE TRYING TO FLEE.

218 AD

DIADUMENIAN IN THE MEANTIME WAS
KILLED BY ELAGABALUS.

222 AD

ELAGABALUS WAS KILLED BY THE
PRAETORIAN GUARD WHILE HIDING
IN A TRUNK WITH HIS MOTHER.

235 AD

SEVERUS ALEXANDER AND HIS MOTHER
WERE KILLED BY THEIR OWN ARMY
WHILE INVADING GERMANY, FOR BRIBING
THE GERMANS TO SURRENDER.

238 AD

MAXIMUS THRAX WAS KILLED IN HIS TENT
BY HIS OWN ARMY, HIS HEAD WAS
MOUNTED ON A CAVALRYMAN'S PIKE,
AND HIS BODY WAS FED TO THE DOGS.

238 AD

PUPIENUS AND BALBINUS, WHO RULED JOINTLY,
WERE FOUND SQUABBLING IN THE IMPERIAL
PALACE BY THE PRAETORIAN GUARD

238 AD

GORDIAN I, UPON LEARNING THAT
HIS SON GORDIAN II HAD LOST THE
BATTLE OF CARTHAGE, HUNG HIMSELF
WITH HIS OWN BELT.

238 AD

GORDIAN II DISAPPEARED DURING THE BATTLE OF CARTHAGE.

244AD

GORDIAN III WAS KILLED
WHILE INVADING IRAQ.

249 AD

PHILIP THE ARAB IS RECKONED BY SOME TO BE THE
FIRST EMPEROR TO DIE A CHRISTIAN, IN BATTLE
AGAINST HIS USURPER DECIUS.

251 AD

DECIUS RULED JOINTLY WITH HIS SON
HERENNIUS ETRUSCUS. THEY PERISHED
TOGETHER IN A SWAMP UNDER A HAIL
OF ARROWS FROM THE GOTHS.

251 AD

HOSTILIAN DIED OF THE PLAGUE.

253 AD

TREBONIANUS GALLUS WHO RULED JOINTLY WITH
HIS SON VOLUSIAN DIED UNDER THE SWORD OF
THEIR OWN ARMY.

253Ab

AEMILIAN WAS KILLED BY HIS OWN SOLDIERS
WHILE CROSSING A BRIDGE, FOR BEHAVING, THEY
SAID, LIKE A COMMON SOLDIER INSTEAD OF
A GENERAL.

260 AD

VALERIAN WAS CAPTURED BY THE
PERSIANS AND IS SAID BY SOME TO HAVE
BEEN SKINNED AND STUFFED WITH MANURE.

GALLIENUS WAS STRUCK DOWN BY A CABAL
OF GENERALS AFTER LEAVING HIS TENT
WITHOUT A BODYGUARD.

269 AD

POSTUMUS WAS KILLED BY HIS SOLDIERS
FOR REFUSING TO LET THEM PILLAGE
IN GERMANY.

270 AD

CLAUDIUS GOTHICUS DIED OF SMALLPOX.

270AD

QUINTILLUS DIED WHILE BEING BLED
BY HIS PHYSICIAN.

274AD

ZENOBIA WAS CHAINED TO A DAIS IN THE HIPPODROME AND BEHEADED.

275AD

AURELIAN WAS ASSASSINATED IN A PLOT HATCHED BY HIS SECRETARY FOR BEING TOO STRICT.

AFTER 275AD

ULPIA SEVERINA, THE ONLY WOMAN TO RULE ALL OF
ROME ON HER OWN, DIED WITHOUT NOTICE.

276 AD

TACITUS DIED IN A FEVER AFTER GOING
INSANE AND THREATENING TO NAME
ALL THE MONTHS OF THE YEAR
AFTER HIMSELF.

276ᴀᴅ

FLORIAN WAS CUT DOWN IN THE
DESERTS OF TURKEY BY HIS OWN
SUNBURNED TROOPS.

282 AD

PROBUS WAS CHASED UP A TOWER AND KILLED BY HIS OWN SOLDIERS AFTER ASKING THEM TO DRAIN A MARSH.

283 AD

CARUS WAS STRUCK BY LIGHTNING.

284 AD

NUMERIAN WAS FOUND DEAD INSIDE HIS COACH
AFTER SUFFERING AN INSOMNIA-INDUCED
INFLAMMATION OF THE EYES.

285AD

CARINUS WAS KILLED AFTER SEDUCING A
TRIBUNE'S WIFE.

CONSTANTIUS CHLORUS DIED AFTER
WAGING WAR IN SCOTLAND.

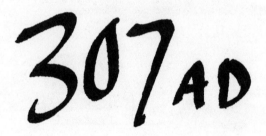

SEVERUS II WAS HELD AS A POLITICAL PRISONER BY
MAXENTIUS, BUT WAS EVENTUALLY KILLED ANYWAY.

310AD

MAXIMINIAN HUNG HIMSELF ON CONSTANTINE'S
SUGGESTION.

3IIAD

GALERIUS DIED OF GANGRENE IN HIS RECTUM.

312 AD

MAXENTIUS DROWNED IN THE TIBER RIVER.

312 AD

DIOCLETIAN DIED IN DESPAIR OF A WASTING
ILLNESS AFTER BECOMING THE FIRST EMPEROR
TO ABDICATE.

313 AD

MAXIMINIUS DAIA DIED OF HEATSTROKE IN THE
MOUNTAINS NEAR TARSUS.

325AD

LICINIUS WAS ACCUSED BY CONSTANTINE
OF CONSPIRING WITH THE GOTHS AND PUT
TO DEATH.

337 AD

CONSTANTINE BY SOME ACCOUNTS POSTPONED
BAPTISM UNTIL HIS DEATHBED IN ORDER TO SIN AS
MUCH AS POSSIBLE BEFOREHAND.

CONSTANTINE II WAS KILLED IN AN AMBUSH
LED BY HIS BROTHER CONSTANS.

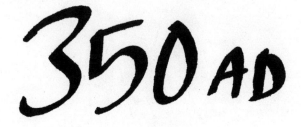

CONSTANS WAS KILLED BY AN AGENT OF
MAGNENTIUS WHILE HIDING IN A TEMPLE
IN THE PYRENEES.

353 AD

MAGNENTIUS WAS PUSHED INTO GAUL BY
CONSTANTIUS II, WHERE, SURROUNDED BY
BARBARIANS, HE CHOSE SUICIDE.

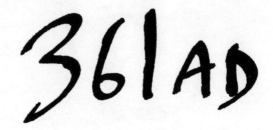

CONSTANTIUS II, FATALLY ILL WHILE BATTLING
HIS USURPER JULIAN, HAD A CHANGE OF
HEART, AND NAMED JULIAN HIS SUCCESSOR.

363 AD

JULIAN WAS STABBED IN THE INTESTINES
WHILE BATTLING THE PERSIANS. HE DIED
OF A HEMORRHAGE AFTER HIS PHYSICIAN
POURED WINE INTO THE WOUND.

364 AD

JOVIAN DIED FROM SMOKE INHALATION WHILE TRYING TO KEEP WARM IN HIS TENT.

375 AD

VALENTINIAN BURST A BLOOD VESSEL
IN HIS HEAD WHILE YELLING
AT GERMAN ENVOYS.

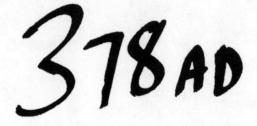

VALENS WAS HIDING IN A SMALL WOODEN HUT
WHEN THE GOTHS SET IT ON FIRE.

383AD

GRATIAN WAS KILLED BY A TURNCOAT WHILE
FLEEING TO THE ALPS.

388 AD

MAGNUS MAXIMUS WAS EXECUTED BY THEODOSIUS FOR APPOINTING HIS INFANT SON CO-EMPEROR.

392 AD

VALENTINIAN II TRIED TO FIRE ONE OF
HIS GENERALS, AN ARROGANT FRANK NAMED
ARBOGAST, AND WAS SOON FOUND
HANGING IN HIS RESIDENCE.

THEODOSIUS DIED OF DROPSY.

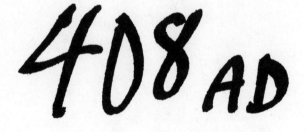

ARCADIUS DIED QUIETLY, HIDDEN AWAY, RARELY
TO BE SEEN, SURROUNDED BY BUREAUCRATIC
HANDLERS, OF NATURAL CAUSES.

411 AD

CONSTANTINE III, FACING A CEASELESS BATTLE OF
SUCCESSION, FLED TO A SANCTUARY TO BE ORDAINED
AS A PRIEST, BUT WAS NEVERTHELESS EVENTUALLY
SEIZED AND EXECUTED BY HONORIUS.

421 AD

CONSTANTIUS III DIED FROM EXHAUSTION.

423 AD

HONORIUS DIED OF DROPSY.

425AD

JOANNES WAS DECAPITATED WHILE RIDING A DONKEY AROUND THE HIPPODROME.

450 AD

THEODOSIUS II FELL OFF A HORSE.

455 AD

VALENTINIAN III WAS BASHED IN THE HEAD BY TWO
SCYTHIANS WHILE PRACTICING ARCHERY. THEN A
SWARM OF BEES CAME AND SUCKED UP ALL HIS BLOOD.

455 AD

PETRONIUS MAXIMUS WAS STONED TO DEATH BY
AN ANGRY MOB.

457 AD

MARCIAN FELL ILL AND DIED AFTER FIVE
MONTHS OF SUFFERING.

457 AD

AVITUS, CONDEMNED TO DEATH BY THE ROMAN
SENATE, DIED OF STARVATION WHILE FLEEING
TO GAUL.

MAJORIAN WAS STRIPPED, BEATEN,
TORTURED, AND BEHEADED.

465 AD

LIBIUS SEVERUS WAS A PUPPET TO THE GERMAN
GENERAL RICIMER, WHO HAD HIM POISONED.

472 AD

ANTHEMIUS WAS BEHEADED IN ST. PETER'S BASILICA BY RICIMER.

472 AD

OLYBRIUS MANAGED TO OUTLIVE RICIMER
ONLY TO DIE OF DROPSY.

474 AD

LEO THE GREAT DIED OF DYSENTERY.

477AD

BASILISCUS WAS IMPRISONED IN A DRIED
UP RESERVOIR WITH HIS FAMILY AND
STARVED TO DEATH.

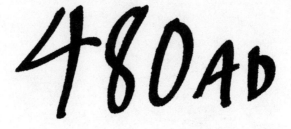

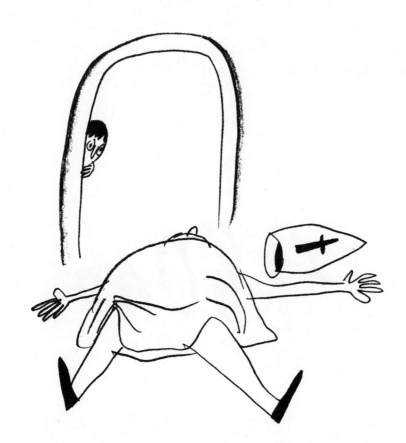

GLYCERIUS WAS DEPOSED AND FLED TO DALMATIA, WHERE HE DIED A BISHOP.

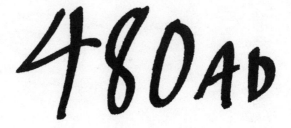

JULIUS NEPOS, HAVING SURVIVED THE COLLAPSE OF THE
WESTERN ROMAN EMPIRE, WAS STABBED IN HIS
VILLA BY A SOLDIER WORKING FOR HIS
PREDECESSOR GLYCERIUS.

ZENO, IN A DRUNKEN STUPOR, WAS BURIED ALIVE BY HIS WIFE ARIADNE.

ROMULUS AUGUSTULUS, THE LAST EMPEROR,
OUTLIVED THE EMPIRE, BUT HIS FATE IS
SOMETHING OF A MYSTERY...